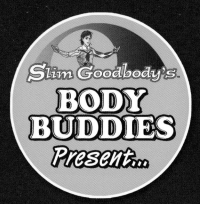

THE MIGHTY MUSCULAR AND SKELETAL SYSTEMS

How do my muscles and bones work?

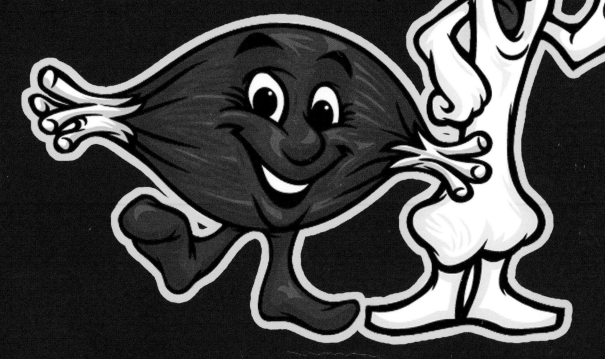

CRABTREE
Publishing Company
www.crabtreebooks.com

Crabtree Publishing Company
www.crabtreebooks.com

Series Development, Writing, and Packaging:
    John Burstein Slim Goodbody Corp.
Medical Reviewer:
    Christine S. Burstein, RN, MSN, FNP
Designer: Tammy West, Westgraphix
Project coordinator: Robert Walker
Editors: Mark Sachner, Water Buffalo Books
    Molly Aloian
Proofreader: Adrianna Morganelli
Production coordinator: Katherine Berti
Prepress technicians: Rosie Gowsell,
    Katherine Berti, Ken Wright
Flex and Strut Character Design and Illustration:
    Mike Ray, Ink Tycoon
Medical Illustrations: Colette Sands, Render Ranch

Picture credits:
© istockphoto: p. 6, 12a
© Shutterstock: cover, p. 7a, 10b, 10c, 10d, 10e, 10f,
    11a, 13, 15a, 17a, 18a, 18b, 20–21, 22a, 23b, 26–27
© Slim Goodbody: p. 7b, 10a, 11b, 12b, 14, 15b,
    15c, 16, 17b, 19, 22b, 24, 25a, 25b, 25c

"Slim Goodbody," "Flex and Strut" and Render Ranch
illustrations, copyright © Slim Goodbody

Acknowledgements:
The author would like to thank the following
children for all their help in this project:
Lucas Burstein, Louisa Crane, Isabella Crane,
Aiden Gordon, Ginny Laurita, Renaissance Lyman,
Yanmei McElhaney, Joshua Montavo

Library and Archives Canada Cataloguing in Publication

Burstein, John
    The mighty muscular and skeletal systems : how do my bones
and muscles work? / John Burstein.

(Slim Goodbody's body buddies)
Includes index.
ISBN 978-0-7787-4433-7 (pbk.).--ISBN 978-0-7787-4419-1 (bound)

    1. Musculoskeletal system--Juvenile literature. I. Title.
II. Series: Burstein, John . Slim Goodbody's body buddies.

QP301.B87 2009   j612.7   C2008-907855-1

Library of Congress Cataloging-in-Publication Data

Burstein, John.
  The mighty muscular and skeletal systems : how do my bones and
muscles work? / John Burstein.
        p. cm. -- (Slim Goodbody's body buddies)
    Includes index.
    ISBN 978-0-7787-4433-7 (pbk. : alk. paper) -- ISBN 978-0-7787-4419-1
(reinforced library binding : alk. paper)
    1. Musculoskeletal system--Juvenile literature. 2. Human
locomotion--Juvenile literature. I. Title. II. Series.

    QP301.B93 2009
    612.7--dc22

                                                        2008052376

Crabtree Publishing Company
www.crabtreebooks.com   1-800-387-7650

Published in Canada
Crabtree Publishing
616 Welland Ave.
St. Catharines, Ontario
L2M 5V6

Published in the United States
Crabtree Publishing
PMB16A
350 Fifth Ave., Suite 3308
New York, NY 10118

Published in the United Kingdom
Crabtree Publishing
White Cross Mills
High Town, Lancaster
LA1 4XS

Published in Australia
Crabtree Publishing
386 Mt. Alexander Rd.
Ascot Vale (Melbourne)
VIC 3032

About the Author
John Burstein (also known as Slim Goodbody) has been entertaining and educating children
for over thirty years. His programs have been broadcast on CBS, PBS, Nickelodeon, USA,
and Discovery. He has won numerous awards including the Parent's Choice Award and the
President's Council's Fitness Leader Award. Currently, Mr. Burstein tours the country with his
multimedia live show "Bodyology." For more information, please visit **slimgoodbody.com**.

CONTENTS

Words in **bold** are defined in the glossary on page 30.

MEET THE BODY BUDDIES

HELLO. MY NAME IS SLIM GOODBODY.

I am very happy that you are reading this book. It means that you want to learn about your body!

I believe that the more you know about how your body works, the prouder you will feel.

I believe that the prouder you feel, the more you will do to take care of yourself.

I believe that the more you do to take care of yourself, the happier and healthier you will be.

To provide you with the very best information about how your body works, I have put together a team of good friends. I call them my Body Buddies, and I hope they will become your Body Buddies, too!

Let me introduce them to you:

- **HUFF AND PUFF** will guide you through the lungs and the respiratory system.

- **TICKER** will lead you on a journey to explore the heart and circulatory system.

- **COGNOS** will explain how the brain and nervous system work.

- **SQUIRT** will let you in on the secrets of tiny glands that do big jobs.

- **FLEX AND STRUT** will walk you through the workings of your bones and muscles.

- **GURGLE** will give you a tour of the stomach and digestive system.

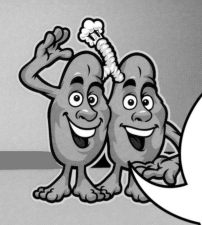

HUFF & PUFF Say...
YOUR RESPIRATORY SYSTEM IS MADE UP OF YOUR LUNGS, ALL THE AIRWAYS CONNECTED WITH THEM, AND THE MUSCLES THAT HELP YOU BREATHE.

TICKER Says...
YOUR CIRCULATORY SYSTEM IS MADE UP OF YOUR HEART, WHICH PUMPS YOUR BLOOD, AND THE TUBES, CALLED BLOOD VESSELS, THROUGH WHICH YOUR BLOOD FLOWS.

COGNOS Says...
YOUR NERVOUS SYSTEM IS MADE UP OF YOUR BRAIN, **SPINAL CORD**, AND ALL THE NERVES IN YOUR BODY.

SQUIRT Says...
YOUR ENDOCRINE SYSTEM IS MADE UP OF MANY DIFFERENT GLANDS THAT PRODUCE SUBSTANCES TO HELP YOUR BODY WORK PROPERLY.

GURGLE Says...
YOUR DIGESTIVE SYSTEM HELPS TURN THE FOOD YOU EAT INTO ENERGY. IT INCLUDES YOUR STOMACH, LIVER, AND INTESTINES.

FLEX & STRUT Say...
YOUR MUSCULAR SYSTEM IS MADE UP OF MUSCLES THAT HELP YOUR BODY MOVE. THE SKELETAL SYSTEM IS MADE UP OF THE BONES THAT HOLD YOUR BODY UP.

TEAMWORK

HI. MY NAME IS FLEX. I AM A MUSCLE.

I HELP MOVE THE BODY AROUND.

HI. MY NAME IS STRUT. I AM A BONE.

I HELP HOLD THE BODY UP.

WE WROTE THIS BOOK TO TEACH YOU ALL ABOUT HOW WE WORK.

WE HAVE DECIDED TO TAKE TURNS TELLING OUR STORIES.

FIRST, STRUT WILL TALK ABOUT BONES.

THEN FLEX WILL TALK ABOUT MUSCLES.

AS YOU READ OUR BOOK, YOU WILL UNDERSTAND WHY WE MAKE SUCH A GREAT TEAM!

BONE CHAMP

You have more bones than your parents! A baby is born with about 300 separate bones. An adult has 206 separate bones. You may wonder how it is possible for a baby to have more bones than a grown-up. The answer is that some bones **fuse**, or join together, as you grow up. For example, babies are born with three separate bones in their upper arms. As babies grow, these three bones fuse into one bone.

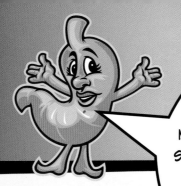

GURGLE says...
MINERALS ARE SUBSTANCES FOUND IN MOST FOOD. YOUR BODY NEEDS MINERALS TO STAY HEALTHY AND STRONG. ONE MINERAL, CALLED CALCIUM, IS ESPECIALLY IMPORTANT FOR BUILDING STRONG BONES.

SKELETON SKILLS

The bones of your body are called the skeleton. Your skeleton does many important jobs:

- It gives your body its shape.

- It holds you up.

- It protects the softer parts inside your body such as your lungs and heart.

- It manufactures blood **cells**.

- It stores up minerals, such as calcium and phosphorus, that can be released at a later time.

JUST A SOFTY

Feel the end of your nose. Move it around a bit. There is cartilage in the end of your nose. Cartilage is a material that is soft and **flexible**. When you were born, many of your bones contained cartilage. That made many of your bones very soft. As you grow, most of your cartilage is slowly replaced by harder bone. Your bones get longer and stronger. It takes about twenty years for this process to be completed. When you are fully grown, some parts of your body will still have cartilage. One of them is your nose.

cartilage

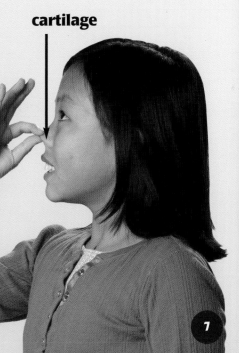

BUSY BONES

SOME PEOPLE THINK THAT BONES ARE ALL DRIED UP.

SOME PEOPLE THINK THAT BONES NEVER CHANGE.

THESE PEOPLE ARE WRONG!

INSIDE YOUR BODY, BONES ARE ALIVE AND GROWING.

LIVING CELLS

Bones are made of living cells. Living cells are always busy. There are three kinds of busy cells in your bones:

1. Osteoblasts are cells that make new bone material and repair damage.

2. Osteoclasts are cells that remove old bone material when it breaks down. They also help shape your bones as they grow.

3. Osteocytes are formed from osteoblasts and help keep the bone strong.

osteocytes

osteoblasts

osteoclast

TICKER says...
YOUR HEART PUMPS BLOOD, WHICH CONTAINS NUTRIENTS. BLOOD CARRIES THESE NUTRIENTS TO YOUR BONES.

BONY LAYERS

Bones need to be lightweight. Heavy bones would make it hard for you to move around. Bones are light because they are not solid through and through. They are built in layers:

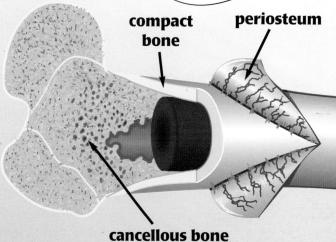

compact bone

periosteum

cancellous bone

1. The periosteum is the very thin **membrane**, or outer layer, covering of the bone. The periosteum contains nerves and blood vessels. Blood brings nutrients to the bones and carries waste away.

2. Compact bone is the next layer of the bone. Compact bone is the smooth, hard outer part of the bone. It looks like ivory and is extremely strong.

3. Cancellous bone is the inner layer. Cancellous bone is also called spongy bone because it looks like a sponge, with many small holes. Spongy bone is not quite as hard as compact bone, but it is still very strong.

BONY BLOOD

Inside the empty spaces of most cancellous, or spongy, bone is **bone marrow**. Bone marrow looks like thick jelly. The marrow manufactures blood cells.

bone marrow

blood cells

GREAT SHAPES

BONES HAVE DIFFERENT SHAPES AND SIZES.

EACH OF US IS DESIGNED TO DO A SLIGHTLY DIFFERENT JOB.

WE ALSO FIT TOGETHER PERFECTLY LIKE THE PIECES OF A JIGSAW PUZZLE.

BONE BASICS

Bones come in four basic shapes:

1. Long bones have a long, thin shaft with two wider ends. Arm and leg bones are long bones.
2. Short bones are small and cube shaped. Wrist bones and ankle bones are short bones.
3. Flat bones are thin, flat, and slightly curved. Your shoulder blade is a flat bone.
4. Irregular bones have unusual shapes. Bones in your spine are irregular bones.

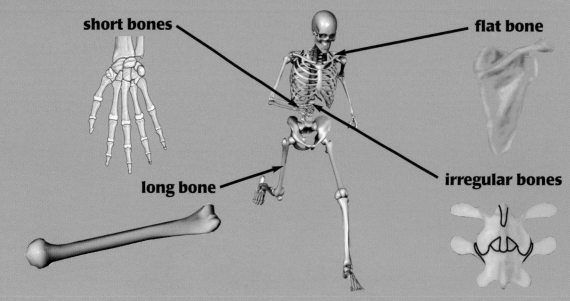

short bones

flat bone

long bone

irregular bones

UP AT THE TOP

There are 22 bones in your skull. Skull bones are divided into two sets:

1. Eight large, flat bones surround your brain. These bones form a thick, hard dome called the **cranium**. Your cranium protects your brain.

2. Fourteen bones form the structure of your face. These bones are called the facial bones. All of your facial bones are fixed in place except your mandible. The mandible is another name for the jawbone.

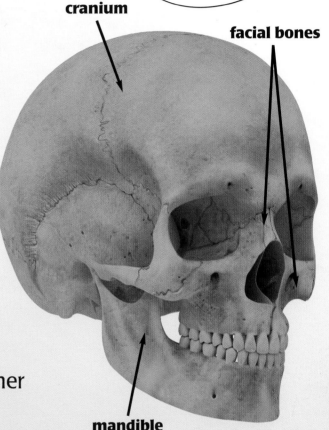

cranium

facial bones

mandible

BE A SCIENTIST

Here is an experiment to help you feel some of your facial bones.

Directions:

1. Place your fingers just beneath your eyes.

2. Press in gently.

You have just felt the edges of the facial bones of your eye sockets.

Here is what you will need:
• Your face
• Your fingers

SUPER SUPPORT

YOUR BACKBONE HOLDS UP YOUR SKULL.

THE BACKBONE IS MADE UP OF SEVERAL BONES THAT ARE ALL IN A LINE.

SHOCK ABSORBERS

Your backbone is also called the spine. The bones that make up your spine are called vertebrae. Vertebrae have an irregular shape. There are small disks of cartilage between each vertebrae. When you are sitting, standing, or even lying still, these disks keep the vertebrae from rubbing against one another. When you walk, run, or jump, the disks cushion your vertebrae so they do not bang into one another.

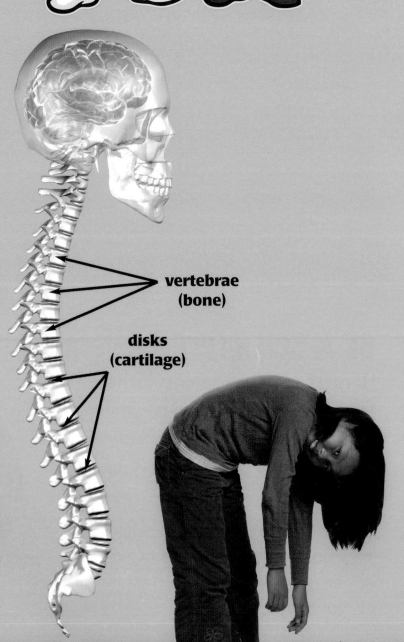

vertebrae (bone)

disks (cartilage)

ALL IN LINE

There are 33 vertebrae in the spine.
Vertebrae are divided into five groups:

1. The top seven vertebrae are called the **cervical**
vertebrae. The cervical vertebrae support your
head and neck.

2. There are twelve **thoracic** vertebrae below
the cervical vertebrae. The thoracic vertebrae
help hold your ribs in place.

3. There are five **lumbar** vertebrae below the
thoracic vertebrae. They support most of
your upper body.

4. The sacrum is below the lumbar vertebrae.
The sacrum is made up of five fused vertebrae.

5. At the bottom of the spine is the coccyx.
Sometimes the coccyx is called the tail
bone. The coccyx is made of four
fused vertebrae.

A BONY BOWL

Your sacrum and coccyx join with your two
hipbones. They form a bony bowl called
your pelvis. Your pelvis helps support the
upper parts of your body. It also protects
some of the **organs** in your lower **abdomen**.

cervical
vertabrae

thoracic
vertabrae

lumbar
vertabrae

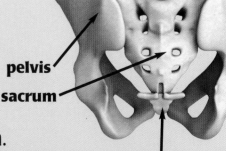

pelvis
sacrum

coccyx

COOL CAGE

BONES ARE STRONG AND HARD.

YOUR HEART AND LUNGS ARE SOFT.

BONES KEEP YOUR HEART AND LUNGS SAFE INSIDE A BONY CAGE.

BUILT OF BONE

Your rib cage is made up of thin, curved, flat bones. There is a strong, flat bone called the sternum at the front of the rib cage. The irregular bones of your spine are at the back of your rib cage. Your rib cage protects your heart and lungs as well as parts of your stomach, spleen, liver, and kidneys.

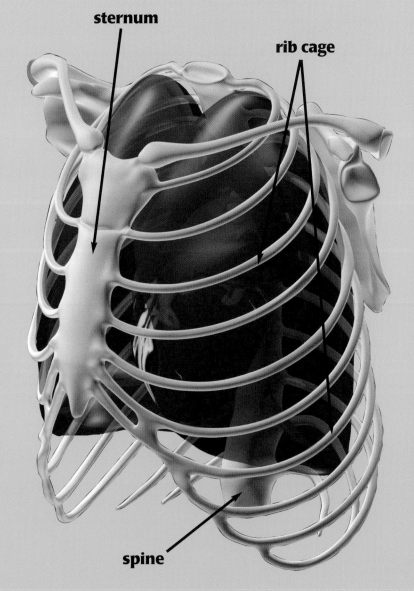

sternum

rib cage

spine

DOUBLE DOZEN

You have twelve pairs of ribs:

- The first seven pairs of rib bones are called the true ribs. True ribs are connected by cartilage directly to the sternum.
- The next three pairs of ribs are called false ribs. False ribs are slightly shorter than the true ribs. They are not attached directly to the sternum. Instead, false ribs are attached by cartilage to the lowest true rib.
- The last two sets of ribs are called floating ribs. Floating ribs are the smallest ribs. They are connected to the spine, but they are not connected to anything in the front.

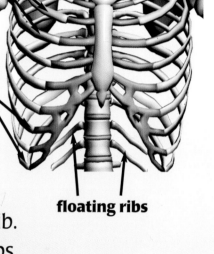

true ribs

false ribs

floating ribs

STRONG SHOULDER

Your shoulder socket is made up of two bones:

1. The scapula, or shoulder bone, on the back side of your rib cage.
2. The clavicle, or collarbone, on the front side of your rib cage.

The ends of your scapula and clavicle meet to form your shoulder socket. Your upper arm bone fits into this socket.

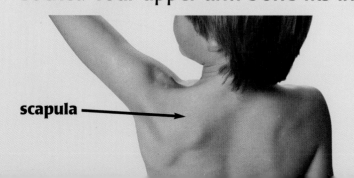

scapula

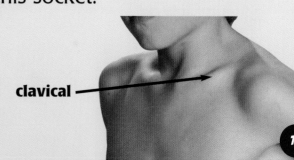

clavical

A BOUNTY OF BONES

MORE THAN HALF OF THE BONES IN YOUR BODY ARE LOCATED IN YOUR ARMS, HANDS, LEGS, AND FEET.

OPEN ARMS

You have three bones in each of your arms:

1. The humerus is the longest bone in your arm. Your humerus is connected to and hangs below your scapula.

2. The ulna is below the humerus.

3. The radius is right next to the ulna. The radius is shorter than the ulna, but it does most of the work when you move your wrist and hand.

The humerus joins with the ulna and the radius to make your elbow joint.

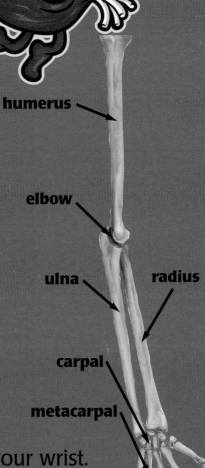

humerus

elbow

ulna

radius

carpal

metacarpal

phalange

HANDY HANDS

Each hand has a total of 27 bones:

• There are eight small carpal bones in your wrist.

• Your palm is made up of five metacarpal bones.

• Your fingers are made up of fourteen bones called phalanges. Each finger has three phalanges. Your thumb has only two phalanges.

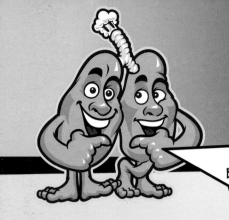

> **HUFF & PUFF say...**
> THE HYOID BONE IS THE ONLY BONE IN YOUR BODY THAT IS NOT CONNECTED TO ANOTHER BONE. IT IS ENTIRELY SUPPORTED BY YOUR NECK MUSCLES AND HELPS SUPPORT YOUR TONGUE.

LONG LEGS

You have four bones in each of your legs:

1. Your femur, or thighbone, is the longest and strongest bone in your body.

2. Your patella, or kneecap, protects the knee joint.

3. Your tibia, or shinbone, is connected to the femur right behind the patella.

4. Your fibula is located right beside the tibia.

FABULOUS FEET

Each foot has 26 bones:

- There are seven small tarsal bones in your ankle. The largest tarsal bone is your heel bone.

- There are five metatarsal bones in your instep.

- There are fourteen phalanges in your toes. All your toes have three phalanges except your big toe, which only has two.

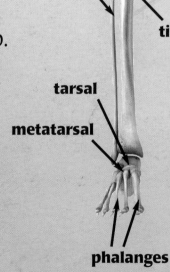

femur

patella

fibula

tibia

tarsal

metatarsal

phalanges

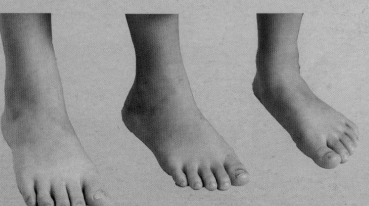

JOINING UP

THE PLACES WHERE BONES MEET ARE CALLED JOINTS.

A JOINT JOINS BONES TOGETHER.

A JOINT IS ALSO SET UP TO KEEP BONES SLIGHTLY SEPARATED. THAT PREVENTS US FROM RUBBING AGAINST EACH OTHER AS WE MOVE.

WHERE BONES MEET BONES

Not all joints work the same way. Some allow the body to move a lot. Some do not allow any movement at all.

There are three basic types of joints in your body:

partially movable joints

1. Immovable joints are the joints between the bones of your skull. Your skull bones fit so tightly together, that almost no movement is possible.

immovable joints

2. Partially movable joints are the joints between your vertebrae. Each joint allows only a little movement, but when they all work together, these joints give your spine a wide range of motion.

3. Synovial joints are found in many places in your body. These joints allow your body to move freely.

SQUIRT says...
THE BONES IN YOUR MOVABLE JOINTS ARE HELD TOGETHER BY LIGAMENTS. LIGAMENTS WORK LIKE VERY STRONG RUBBER BANDS.

SYNOVIAL JOINT JOBS

There are several kinds of synovial joints:

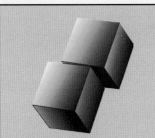

Gliding joints allow you to bend, stretch, and circle your wrist.

The pivot joint at your neck allows your head to move from side to side.

Saddle joints allow your thumbs to rock back and forth and from side to side.

Hinge joints at your elbows, knees, and some of your fingers and toes allow back and forth movement like the opening and closing of a door.

Ball and socket joints at your hips and shoulders allow the greatest amount of movement in the body.

A BONY PICTURE

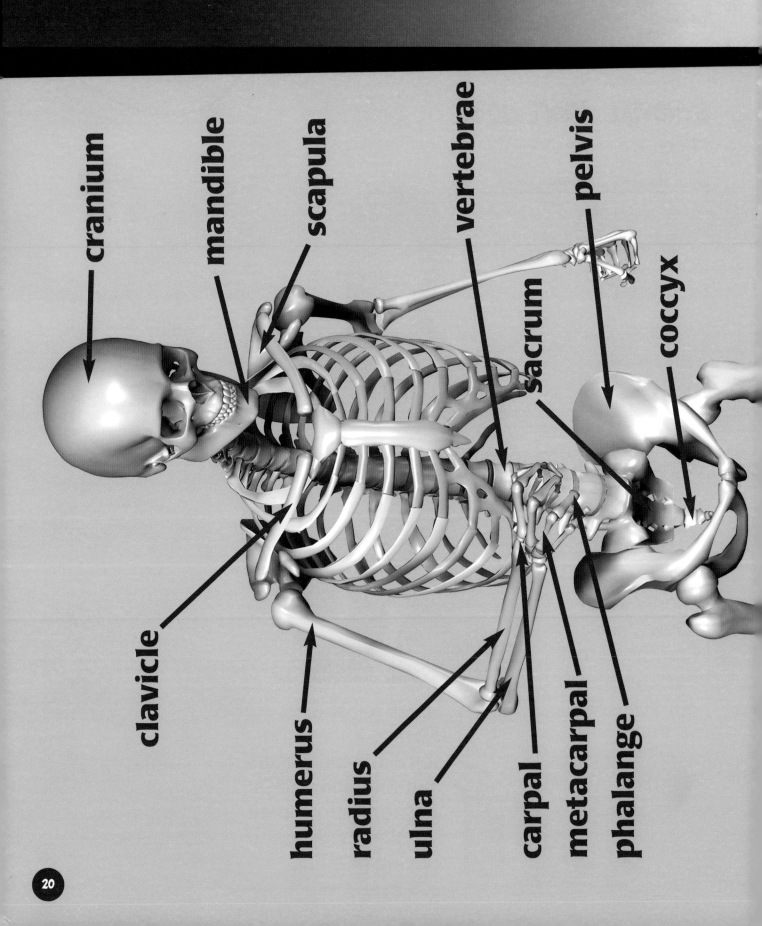

cranium

mandible

scapula

vertebrae

pelvis

sacrum

coccyx

clavicle

humerus

radius

ulna

carpal

metacarpal

phalange

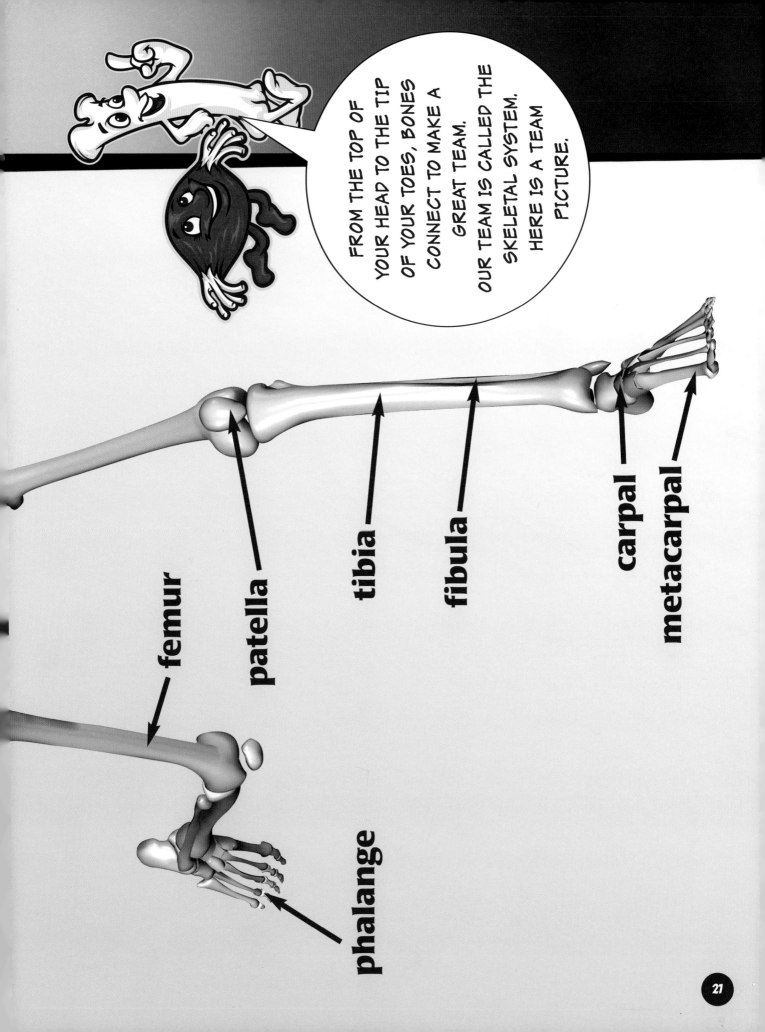

21

MUSCLE MOTION

BONES CANNOT MOVE BY THEMSELVES. MUSCLES GET THE BODY MOVING.

THERE ARE OVER 650 OF US AT WORK IN YOUR BODY.

SOME OF US MOVE LONG BONES SO YOU CAN WALK.

SOME OF US MOVE SHORT BONES SO YOU CAN WRITE.

SOME OF US MOVE YOUR FLAT BONES SO YOU CAN CHEW.

SOME OF US MOVE IRREGULAR BONES SO YOU CAN BEND OVER.

striped muscle

BONE MOVERS

The muscles that move your bones are called skeletal muscles. Skeletal muscles are voluntary muscles. That means you can control what they do. For example, your arm will not lift unless you want it to. Skeletal muscles are made of muscle fibers. Some of these muscle fibers are light, and some are dark. Under a microscope, skeletal muscles look striped.

TICKER says...
SKELETAL MUSCLES ARE ATTACHED TO BONES BY TOUGH BANDS OF MATERIAL CALLED TENDONS. IF YOU WIGGLE YOUR FINGERS AND LOOK AT THE TOP OF YOUR HAND, THE ROPE-LIKE BANDS YOU SEE ARE TENDONS.

MORE MUSCLES

You have two other kinds of muscles besides skeletal muscles:

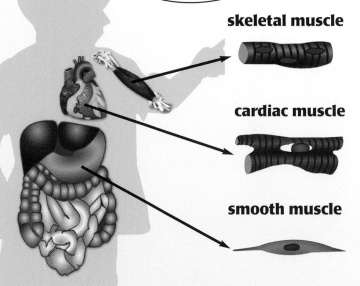

skeletal muscle

cardiac muscle

smooth muscle

1. Smooth muscles are found in the walls of your blood vessels, intestines, stomach, and other organs. You do not tell smooth muscles what to do. They work automatically. Smooth muscles are also made of fibers, but these fibers look smooth, not striped.

2. Cardiac muscle is only found in your heart. Cardiac muscle is also an involuntary muscle. It looks like smooth muscle, but it can work longer and harder than any other muscle in the body.

FACE IT

The muscles in your face are skeletal muscles, but they are not all attached to bones. Many facial muscles are attached to other muscles or to the skin. This allows the muscles to pull on your skin and make very small movements that change your expressions.

POWERFUL PAIRS

MUSCLES WORK IN PAIRS.

ONE MUSCLE PULLS A BONE IN ONE DIRECTION.

THE OTHER MUSCLE PULLS THE BONE BACK.

KEEPING MUSCLES BUSY

To move bones, muscles must contract. Muscles bunch up when they contract. They get thicker and shorter. When a muscle contracts, it pulls the bone it is attached to and the bone moves.

Once the muscle has pulled the bone, it relaxes. The bone stays in place until another muscle contracts and pulls the bone back. One muscle does the bending. The other muscle does the straightening.

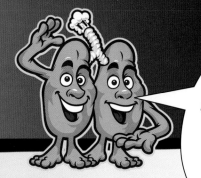

HUFF &
PUFF say...
AEROBIC EXERCISES
LIKE JOGGING OR BIKE
RIDING MAKE YOUR
MUSCLES USE
MORE OXYGEN.

THE ACTION OF CONTRACTION

Muscles are able to contract because muscle cells contain many microscopic fibers called myofilaments. When a muscle is relaxed, the myofilaments overlap each other a tiny bit. When a muscle contracts, the myofilaments slide past each other until they completely overlap. This makes the muscle shorter and thicker.

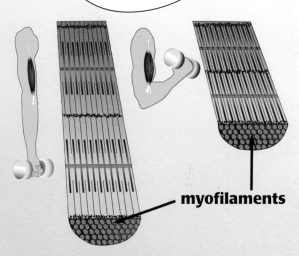

myofilaments

BE A SCIENTIST

To understand more about how muscles work in pairs, try this experiment.

Here is what you will need:
- Your left arm
- Your right hand

Directions:

1. Hold your left arm out straight and place your right hand on your left biceps muscle.

2. Bend your arm. You will feel your bicep contracting.

3. Once your arm is bent, relax your biceps. Do not contract any other muscle. What happens?

4. Place your right hand on your left triceps. The triceps is the muscle at the back side of your upper arm.

5. Feel your triceps contract to bring the arm straight.

   Muscles work in pairs so you can move freely and easily.

MARVELOUS MUSCLES

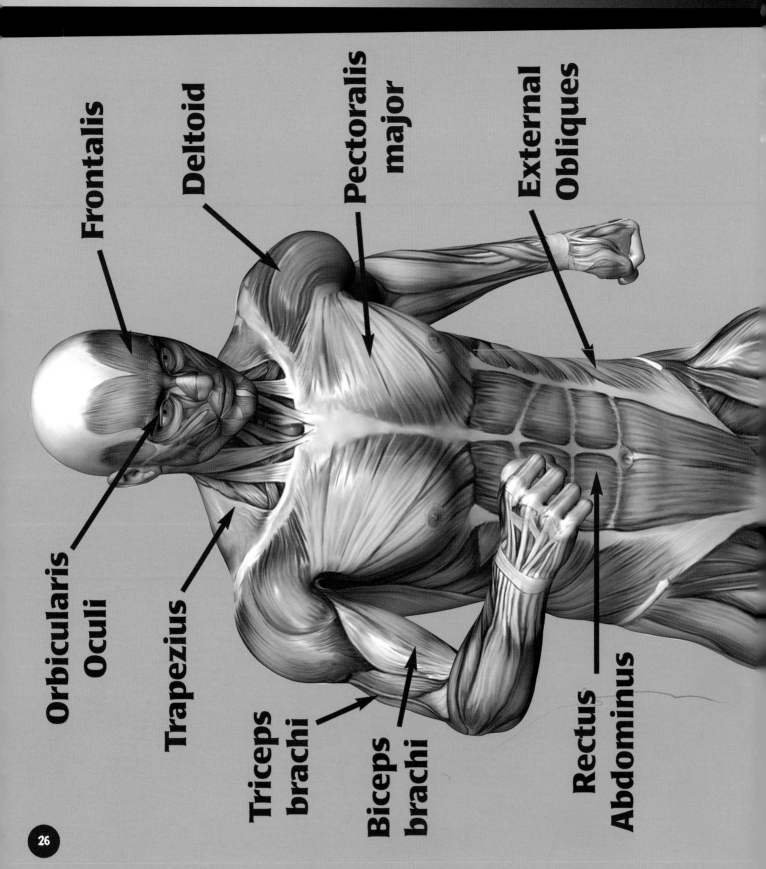

Frontalis

Deltoid

Pectoralis major

External Obliques

Orbicularis Oculi

Trapezius

Triceps brachi

Biceps brachi

Rectus Abdominus

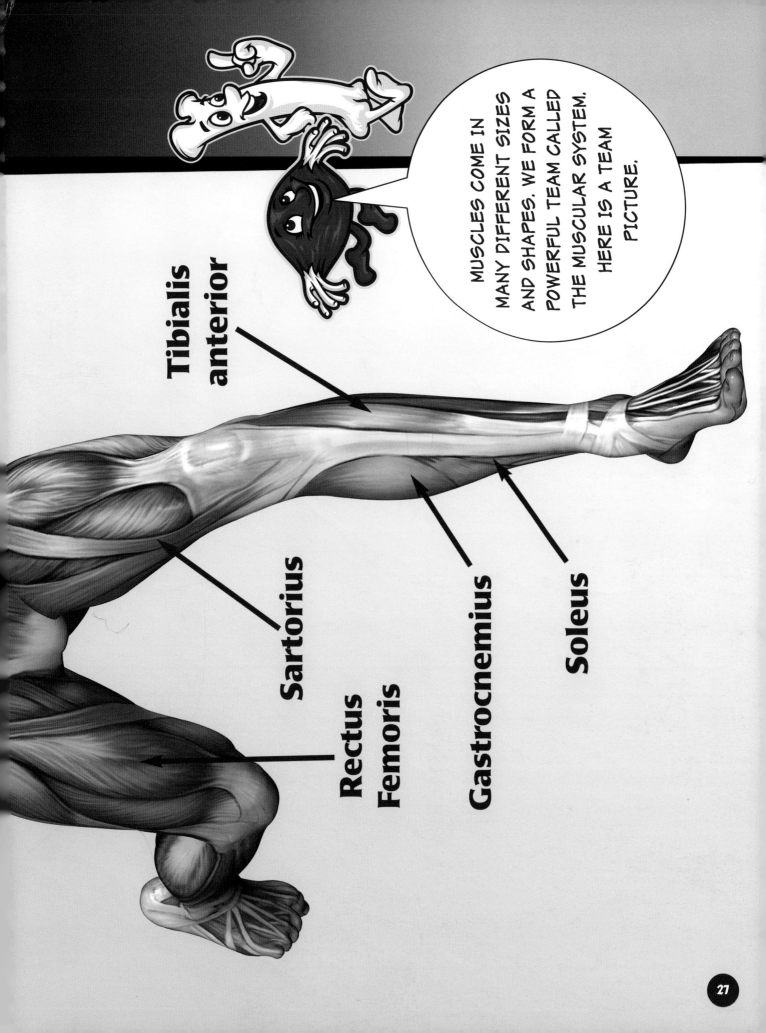

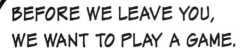

BEFORE WE LEAVE YOU,
WE WANT TO PLAY A GAME.

IN THE BOX BELOW YOU WILL SEE
EIGHT PHRASES.

EACH PHRASE HAS THE WORD "BONE" IN IT.

WE WILL START A SENTENCE AND YOU TRY TO
FILL IN THE BLANK USING ONE OF THE PHRASES.

FOR EXAMPLE, IF SENTENCE NUMBER 1 IS:
IF YOU LIKE TO LIE AROUND DOING NOTHING,
PEOPLE MIGHT CALL YOU A _____.

YOU WOULD CHOOSE THE PHRASE "A":
"LAZYBONES." GOT IT?

Remember, choose a phrase that completes the sentence. The right matches of sentences and phrases are at the bottom of the page. But you will have to turn the book upside down to read them!

1. If you like to lie around doing nothing, people might call you _____.

2. If you are angry with someone, you might have a _____ with that person.

3. A foolish person is sometimes called a _____.

4. When you study really hard, you _____ on the subject.

5. If you are afraid to stand up for yourself, people might say you have no _____.

6. Another name for a cemetery is a _____.

7. A doctor who operates on people is sometimes called a _____.

A. lazybones	**C.** bone yard	**E.** bonehead	**G.** bone to pick
B. bone up	**D.** backbone	**F.** sawbones	

ANSWERS: 1-A, 2-G, 3-E, 4-B, 5-D, 6-C, 7-F

Amazing Facts About Your Skeletal and Muscular Systems

MUSCLES MAKE UP ABOUT ONE-HALF OF YOUR BODY WEIGHT.

ABOUT ONE-THIRD OF LIVING BONE IS MADE OF WATER.

THE SMALLEST MUSCLE IN YOUR BODY IS THE STAPEDIUS. IT MOVES THE STAPES BONE IN YOUR MIDDLE EAR.

EYE MUSCLES ARE THE BUSIEST MUSCLES IN THE BODY. SCIENTISTS BELIEVE THEY MOVE MORE THAN 100,000 TIMES A DAY!

YOUR BONE MARROW PRODUCES ABOUT 2.6 MILLION RED BLOOD CELLS EVERY SECOND.

THE CLAVICLE IN THE SHOULDER IS THE MOST COMMONLY BROKEN BONE IN THE BODY.

HUMANS AND GIRAFFES HAVE THE SAME NUMBER OF BONES IN THEIR NECKS.

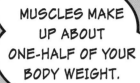

BETWEEN THE AGES OF 50 AND 55, PEOPLE START GETTING SHORTER BECAUSE THE DISKS BETWEEN THEIR VERTEBRAE BEGIN TO FLATTEN.

THE SMALLEST BONE IS THE STAPES BONE IN YOUR MIDDLE EAR. IT IS ONLY ABOUT ONE-TENTH OF AN INCH (2.5 CM) LONG.

THE LONGEST BONE IN YOUR BODY IS YOUR FEMUR. IT IS ABOUT ONE-QUARTER OF YOUR HEIGHT.

MOST PEOPLE HAVE 12 PAIRS OF RIBS, BUT SOME PEOPLE ARE BORN WITH ONE OR MORE EXTRA RIBS, AND SOME PEOPLE MIGHT HAVE ONE PAIR FEWER.

GLOSSARY

abdomen The part of the body, often called the belly, that contains the digestive organs

bone marrow A soft, fatty, jelly-like substance found inside bones that makes blood cells

cells The smallest units, or structures, that make up the body. Cells are so tiny that they cannot be seen without a microscope

cervical Relating to or having to do with the neck

cranium The skull, especially the parts that enclose the brain

flexible Able to be bent without breaking

fuse To blend or join together

lumbar Relating to or having to do with the lower part of the back

membrane A thin layer that forms a covering, lining, or boundary of a structure

nutrients Sources of nourishment and energy, especially from the food we eat

organs Body parts, such as the heart, liver, or lungs, that perform certain functions

spinal cord The bundle of nerves that runs through from the brain through the backbone and branches out through the rest of the body

thoracic Relating to or having to do with the thorax — the part of the body between the neck and the abdomen that includes the rib cage and makes up the chest

FOR MORE INFORMATION

BOOKS

The Skeletal and Muscular System (Body Systems). Sue Barraclough. Heinemann Library.

Skeletal And Muscular System (The Facts on File Illustrated Guide to the Human Body). Lionel Bender (editor). Facts on File.

The Skeletal and Muscular System (Understanding the Human Body). Elaine Wood and Pamela Walker. Lucent Books.

The Skeletal and Muscular Systems (Reading Essentials in Science). Susan Glass. Perfection Learning.

WEBSITES

Discovery Kids

yucky.discovery.com/flash/body/pg000124.html
This website has a lot of information and very cool "yucky" interactive games to play.

Kidhealth

kidshealth.org/kid/htbw/bones.html
Check out this website for a ton of information about your bones and muscles. Learn how to keep them healthy.

Slim Goodbody

www.slimgoodbody.com
Discover loads of fun and free downloads for kids, teachers, and parents.

ThinkQuest

library.thinkquest.org/28807/data/skm.htm
A really fun site with a lot of information about your skeletal and muscular systems.

INDEX

Printed in the U.S.A. - CG